MW00623189

MORE PRAISE FOR

DIVINE, DIVINE, DIVINE

In this startling collection of poems, Daniel B. Summerhill holds two images up to the light and beckons us to examine them: the black body, alive; and the black body, dead. In the titular poem, "Divine, Divine, Divine", the speaker begins with this declaration: "Aint no mama allowing their baby to swing from a tree without divine permission." It is in this vein that we carefully lift, with the author's guidance, the curtain on being black in America; we see, simultaneously, the devastation of mothers whose sons are lynched for being black and, in the imagery of 'swinging' (as opposed to 'hanging') – as if alluding to the old American Spiritual "Swing Low Sweet Chariot" – the divinity, the heart-breaking beauty of choiceless surrender. The final line of this opening poem offers respite:

> besides they'll see
> how beautiful he's become // & be ashamed.

Here, the poem's speaker offers consolation in the sentiment that the beauty of blackness does not end in death but begins anew there. Just as we usher in new life with song, we also say farewell to the departed with song. The allusion to music is a thread that holds together the contrasting images that appear throughout the collection, drawing the reader into not only a nostalgic reverence of African American church tradition in the references to familiar charismatic praise songs, but also the disconcerting reality that those who lift their hands in praise are equally capable of lifting them to inflict pain on others. In the poem "Dialects of Praise", the speaker offers us the offending truth:

> Gold-plated cufflinks anchor the hands
> that left my sister's neck pink
>
> one night prior. His rehearsed tongue
>   yielding-   *Oh Happy Day,*
> when he washed the blood away
>
>   from his hands
> *Waymaker,* just before palms become fist
>   and he sends invocation.
>
> Each song, a tithe.

In the poem "While the Praise Team Sings How Great", we are offered another saddening truth; that even as the abusive chorister in "Dialects of Praise" cannot sing away his sin or offer a verbal tithe as apology, a black boy cannot bury his pain in song:

> he doesn't know how to listen
>   to the gospel without his eyes
> singing songs his heart
>   wished it didn't know

In the poem "When a People Mourn" there is a response to the issue of pain, as if speaking directly to the boy crying in the church pews, unable to join in the singing. In his mourning he can find what the speaker here has discovered in the weaponization of prayer; that if we cannot fight back with our hands, we can at least pull them together in our quest for relief:

There is no blueprint for pain.

Each time a prayer is said,
It is half Psalm, half arrow.
As much blade as it is a promise

Throughout this collection, the author offers a well-balanced narrative. Summerhill's skill lies in his ability to hold both sides of a story with equal dexterity; in the images he presents to us through the speakers in his poems, he juxtaposes what at first seems ordinary to the untrained eye with reality, which is always more sinister upon close inspection. By highlighting through a young boy's lens the cruel reality of growing up black in America we see the following: The beauty of childhood friendships built in an imperfect neighbourhood is juxtaposed with the ominous threat of the gentrification of the same, while the innocence of making memories while playing with friends on the school playground is held up to the light alongside the soul-shattering reality of racism. This author's work forces us to examine that which is uncomfortable to look at, without flinching, because the malice we encounter is embedded in the beauty we were already looking at, like a thorn among the roses.

In the poem "The Time David Misspoke", the speaker brings us into a scene where a boy named David uses the N-word and is acquitted, with words such as "possessed" and "misspoke" telling us that he was not duly punished. However, the black boys who are held in detention for trying to sink David's body in their fists serve their seven-hour-a-day sentences and the speaker asserts that it was "more of a block party than a punishment", a boyishly optimistic take on an unfair situation. This poem seems to say "This is America" in that the black boys somehow know they will contend with many other David figures in their lives:

Bodies like David's

never drown, they just find
new land to colonize.

In "Baritone Body", the author's incredible talent is showcased in a poem which works on the page just as well as it would on the stage as a spoken word piece. The alliteration of the letter "B" allows the poem to convey simply, and with an unforgiving echo, what the entire collection tries to tell us through the speakers' anecdotes and scenarios: "black bodies, black boys, broke, broken, breaking." The poem declares "breaking news!" in the manner of American news headlines announcing that yet another black boy has lost his life in a senseless killing, and the reporter seems to be an older version of the playground David we encounter in the collection, asserting our earlier suspicion that there is something ominous looming behind the boys' survival of this early trauma.

In the poem titled "A Song about Death", the speaker notes that even the sun is a potential enemy:

                The way it peeks cumulous
        as if to say—
                Bury yourself
                in the ground
                once more before
        I burn
        you alive.

In the last poem of the collection lies a simple declaration: "Mama gave me a biblical name", and it is as if we have come full circle here, in that the divine intervention sought in the titular poem can be found in naming a black boy Daniel, in the assertion that who his mother says he is, is who he is, and that is enough. This declaration is almost like the signature couplet in a ghazal, where the poet finally announces his presence to the reader. The poems in this collection are a powerful pushback on the way that the narrative is shifted after the "breaking news" of a black boy's death is declared in mainstream media: there is a digging into the past, an excavation of mistakes, as if to justify the unjustifiable act of taking the life of an innocent person. With the words "I will call you by your name and nothing else", the speaker in this poem strips the power from any entity that aims to name a black boy anything other than what he is and always will be, whether dead or alive: "Divine, Divine, Divine."

NKATEKO MASINGA

poet, Ebedi International Writers Residency Fellow
author of *The Heart is a Caged Animal*

NOMADIC PRESS

OAKLAND

111 FAIRMONT AVENUE
OAKLAND, CA 94611

BROOKLYN

475 KENT AVENUE #302
BROOKLYN, NY 11249

WWW.NOMADICPRESS.ORG

MASTHEAD

FOUNDING AND MANAGING EDITOR
J. K. FOWLER

ASSOCIATE EDITOR
MICHAELA MULLIN

EDITOR
NOELIA CERNA

DESIGN
JEVOHN TYLER NEWSOME

MISSION STATEMENT

Through publications, events, and active community participation, Nomadic Press collectively weaves together platforms for intentionally marginalized voices to take their rightful place within the world of the written and spoken word. Through our limited means, we are simply attempting to help right the centuries' old violence and silencing that should never have occurred in the first place and build alliances and community partnerships with others who share a collective vision for a future far better than today.

INVITATIONS

Nomadic Press wholeheartedly accepts invitations to read your work during our open reading period every year. To learn more or to extend an invitation, please visit: www.nomadicpress.org/invitations

DISTRIBUTION

Orders by teachers, libraries, trade bookstores, or wholesalers:

Small Press Distribution
1341 Seventh Street
Berkeley, California 94701
spd@spdbooks.org
(510) 524-1668 / (800) 869-7553

Divine, Divine, Divine

© 2021 by Daniel B. Summerhill

All rights reserved. No part of this book may be reproduced or transmitted in any form or by any means, electronic or mechanical, without written permission from the publisher.

Requests for permission to make copies of any part of the work should be sent to: info@nomadicpress.org.

This book was made possible by a loving community of chosen family and friends, old and new.

For author questions or to book a reading at your bookstore, university/school, or alternative establishment, please send an email to info@nomadicpress.org.

Cover artwork by Amen'auset Shotlow-Turner (Collage Art & Design)

Published by Nomadic Press, 111 Fairmount Avenue, Oakland, California 94611

First printing, 2021

Printed in the United States of America

Library of Congress Cataloging-in-Publication Data

Title: *Divine, Divine, Divine*

p. cm.

Summary: *Divine, Divine, Divine* by Daniel B. Summerhill is an exploration of the divine and the deviant. A consideration of the Black tongue as a home. Life and death through the lense of language. This collection is an ode to the experiences that make us whole and an acknowledgment of those things that fracture us.

[1. Black History. 2. Black Men. 3. Poetry. 4. Storytelling. 5. Spirituality. 6. Childhood Trauma. 7. Family. 8. American General..] I. III. Title.

LIBRARY OF CONGRESS CONTROL NUMBER: 2021936198

ISBN: 978-1-955239-01-1

DIVINE DIVINE DIVINE

DANIEL B. SUMMERHILL

DIVINE DIVINE DIVINE

DANIEL B. SUMMERHILL

NOMADIC PRESS

contents

acknowledgements

classroom guide

foreword

Iain Haley Pollock once told me and a workshop of fellow poets, including Daniel Summerhill, to write dangerous poems. What proves more dangerous than the poem that challenges its nature? More dangerous than the poet who interrogates a language of oppression to reimagine himself and his people through words? Or as Tim Seibles asks in the introduction to this collection *Buffalo Head Solo*, "Why not a rambunctious and reckless poetry, when the ascendant social order permits nearly every type of corruption and related hypocrisy? Why not risk everything, at least more often if not always?"

Dangerous, rambunctious, reckless: these words embody the ethos of Summerhill's *Divine, Divine, Divine,* a collection of poems that lives within but then discombobulates the nature of language. Summerhill's debut collection presents the chaos and creativity possible when we repurpose the colonial and oppressive history of the English language for Blackness.

This interrogation is not just an outward action in *Divine, Divine, Divine.* The collection also asks for accountability from its speakers. The opening poem "concerning: fire" ends with the line "hard to imagine being on the wrong side / of all this smoke." Authority in this line and the preceding lines derives from a voice that has seen the other side of the smoke. When James Baldwin told Dr. Kenneth Clark in 1963 about the dilemma of the American Negro—being "a little bit colored and a little bit white ... in the head and in the heart"—this is the sentiment that Summerhill investigates in his poems.

Consider the poem "in defense of specific." The poem's list denotes the importance of precision, which in turn, argues the speaker's desire for correctness in a peer pronouncing "specific." Yet as the bracketed section of the poem shows, the speaker offering these examples in the list must confront how doing so out of a love of language and memory of home still doesn't absolve the speaker of participating in the colonial nature of English.

pacific! as thick as her position, the stoop we sat on buried itself and 106th street laid still, as did my posture, attempting to decode her tongue. the quarrel over the word: specific, left my mouth lusting for the body of water she referred to.

In the end, the speaker yields. Despite the personal stake, despite the correctness, he yields. However, the concession is not out of a sense of futility. It's the kindred spirit of Blackness. It's what Terrance Hayes means in his poem "Lighthead's Guide to the Galaxy" when he mentions his father's way of pronouncing "the street" as "discrete." It's the acknowledgement of mutual struggle against oppression that then leans into praise of how the magic of Black imagination allows us to think beyond the borders of proper spelling and grammar to create our poetry.

As Kevin Young writes in *The Grey Album*, this imaginative power liberates Black peoples from our confinement. Summerhill's debut collection wields this power to reinvent every aspect of the poem for Blackness. Whether it's repurposing the sonnet's legacy for a personal history on hip hop or the collection's lack of capitalization to craft its own sense of formality, *Divine, Divine, Divine* is as dangerous as books of poetry can be and more.

In a separate interview with The New York Times, Baldwin said we write to change the world. Even in minor cases, how we alter perspectives through writing is part of that change. By the time you finish *Divine, Divine, Divine*, you, too, will understand not only which side of the smoke you stand on, but also how much of it surrounds you.

QUINTIN COLLINS
author of *The Dandelion Speaks of Survival*
associate director of The Solstice MFA in
Creative Writing Program

introduction

My grandfather was a carpenter, which meant he could make magic with his bare hands. I once watched as he split a two-by-four in half to build the front and rear axles of my go cart. I was 7 and languaging. This lesson was on etymology. I knew english, like prison, didn't add up, when I realized the term saw dust pays more credence to the destroyer than the destruction. I realized saws didn't have dust at all, just blades. And dust was only dust because it was at the bottom, the same way Ta-Nehisi Coates explains, "Black is just someone's name for being at the bottom." I didn't see this as a metaphor for language in '98, but I did when I set out to write these poems many years later. The dust being my language. My language being my body.

In this collection, I explore this metaphor through the lense of East and West Oakland in the early 2000s, through the beat of east 14th, and the trauma of adolescence. I hope to magnify a Black boys proximity with death, God, A Tribe Called Quest, and Shakespeare. I hope to let the homies in through the backdoor in these poems. To sing and celebrate the time mitigating our low hanging pants and Air Force 1 crease-preventing walks. I hope there's a prayer in these pages that allows them to talk to God in whatever language they feel comfortable with.

There are many ways we share experience, and music is among the greatest— Biggie or Pac or Frank or KDot, in particular. The "we" in "we gon' be alright" lets us know Blackness is not monolithic. Our music sings our glory. These poems showcase Black as a congregation, a collective of fists, each with

enough holy to grab heaven by the throat. These pages offer the blacktop as a communal space to make sense of fire, entrepreneurship, retribution, and revelation.

Poems know what they want to be and how they want to arrive there. In *Divine, Divine, Divine,* it is the BART train, or a mongoose bicycle with a busted chain, and a boy learning how to speak while riding them both. A boy who knows his name and knows what his mother's lips mean when they discharge it each time. A boy who recalculates his worth each time a Black body stops breathing. A boy who believes in survival as a tool for vengeance. Survival as salvation.

What is more divine than a non-dying thing? My people die but never die. Our bodies may go but our tongues don't. Language is proof that we're alive. Proof that we're divine.

DANIEL B. SUMMERHILL

concerning: fire

i can hardly imagine all of this rage going
to waste, how our bodies are anti-combustible

anyway. hard to imagine us feeling remorse
for fire our skin has always been glazed in,

a kind of clay we have claimed as skin, or kin.
a rage we've claimed as kin.

hard to imagine any other way of shedding light
on injustice but through brimstone. heat

and equality are fundamental rights and right
now i choose to fan this flame. been brewing

for years— yesterday was kindle. sometimes
all we need is to weep until our wells dry—

other times, all we have left is fire and we'll burn
anything attempting to put out our flame.

hard to imagine being on the wrong side
of all this smoke—

if it brings me to my knees,
it's a bad religion

—frank ocean

divine, divine, divine

ain't no mama allowing their baby to swing
from a tree without divine permission // asked
the coroner to tuck the revolution in his size
six sneakers // asked the mortician to embalm
his face, nobody'll care if the swelling goes
down // nobody'll care if the swelling goes
down, but mama says nobody'll care
if the swelling goes down // ain't no mama
mourning tomorrow // tonight— will have
to do // tomorrow'll be a sort of minstrel
show // & ain't nobody gon' be laughing then
// besides, they'll see how beautiful he's become
// & be ashamed.

glossolalia

i learned how to understand tongue
on 23rd street. through my window,
7:00 am saint vincent depaul
collected its share of hunger.
after a meal, a thickly clothed man,
silver-brown hair, dilated eyes fighting
for their last ounce of white, argued
with whomever or whatever was
near. mornings always welcomed
his bawl. a tenor mostly empty
in its attempt to sing its story. half-
pronounced syllable, a mutter
clawing its way out of his mouth,
a chewed phonic blend. urge to belch
before becoming, before he had
anything comprehendible to say—

dialects of praise

offering envelope, i stick to day-old gum,
      during the break
of the choir director's direction.

      beside me, the sound a sinner
makes. gold-plated cufflinks anchor the hands
      that left my sister's neck pink

one night prior. his rehearsed tongue
      yielding—   *oh happy day,*
when he washed the blood away

      from his hands
waymaker,   just before palms become fists
      and he sends an invocation.

each song, a tithe
      envelope i stick to the gum
between the pews.

say— fuck

say—   those palms hold dirt like cracked
flowerpots. say—   beneath gnats playing hopscotch

in mid-air. say—   those lips hurled fuck as if it were
holy. say—   a prayer strong enough to sin with.

say—   pray for that mouth and how it knows
no other way to rejoice. how it drinks

scotch through a straw, slow. say—   that bastard
was a minister and spat when he talked. say—

he spoke in parables, and never made sense
or say—   always. say— mental math, how we

could see his mind working, but never seen
the steps to get there. say—   we felt

the results in every scar mama birthed. say—
we did not   speak of conception. say—

we did not speak.

grown folk' conversation

          miles mumbles
like a garbage disposal
          as it chews up
the stretched day
          a family has left
behind each dinner time.
          points his head
towards the lego-clustered
          floor, its half-built
houses and plays
          hopscotch on his way
down the hallway
          to his room. his voice,
the scar tissue
          collected from *talking*
too much during grown
          folk's conversation
two nights earlier. from now
          on, it unravels itself
during 9 am recess talks

on what the word "fuck"

means each time

it's discharged. the talks—

their menthol,

their wings

preface before discourse on location

fight the power	Black fist
sign of agreement	Black fist
greeting another Black person	Black fist
peace	Black fist
war	Black fist
to use the bathroom in american lakes pre-k class:	Black fist

[my earliest memories of language came while wiggling to keep from pissing myself. mouth muzzled as custom was to utilize our fingers instead. thumb between my index and middle finger meant *pee*, while a clenched fist signaled a longer trip to the boy's room. the latter always confused me, as the first time i happened upon a Black fist: my sister was watching a documentary on huey newton and bobby seale. her 19-year-old approach to teaching a four-year-old about the Black panthers involved fist only.   many of them.]

shakespeare teaches a lesson on q-tip

never made to read shakespeare or blake,
i'da had to ride through a couple cities
and a busted chain to find the nearest copy.
my canon: mtv, pac's alternative rhyme,

a tribe called quest's re-imagined narrative.
brenda and her baby, my mother and i, six girls
on our block have no idea who ophelia is
or how they become synonyms every time

a razor slit reveals itself. still— every time i sit
in english class, my body becomes truant,
my mind takes flight to 1998, the first time i heard
midnight marauders, q-tip was spittin' a sixteen

that shook my body electric. its current, my canon:
the only thing worth critically thinking about.

all of the others
seek refuge

here. in this pit of a body

    some sort of kinship

or calvary. imagine this

    failed vessel

attempting to corral

    the waves

imagine these bones

    a catalyst

for everything but

    themselves.

how they unfurl across

    the atlantic

time and time again.

    staying afloat.

concerning: survival

any nigga that survives this nightmare, is my goddammed hero...

          –dave chappelle

i apologize mr. chappelle, but i didn't

plan on being brave today just driftwood

the sun is out and that's reason enough

   for me to feel like a champion and i must

admit, i've always wanted to wear a mask

but figure i got my father's nose and ain't

no mask Blacker than that a body forged

   in war will always hunger for a language

unviolent enough to sing inthis blues

   is called

      survival

aunt georgia makes
fried chitlins

being Black takes a certain kind
        of magic to trick
generations into believing
there is a recipe
        to make intestines useful
for something
        other than transporting
shit.
        even when the body
        breaks down food,
it is sure
        to disregard the scraps,
the poison.
how then have we been able
        to take bile
and digest it? to salt
        the distaste
of *nigger*,
        drop the e and r,
adding an a

and spitting out

brother. the same way

we took grits

and made them edible

too.

how to salt a wound

in a classroom full
    of einstein and fitzgerald
posters, you survived
    the inflammation of 9th grade
literature by biting your tongue
    and watching your language
drip to the floor.

kumi and i freestyle

                didn't read   *lord of the flies.*

during sustained silent reading time,

           practiced   rhyming *nigga* with *nigga.*

like rappers do in their songs,

                  the biggest discovery since autotune,

& kanye west's 808s and heartbreak.

an afro pick   with a Black power fist

        find home in an oily scalp.

our air force one sneakers

        walk like frankenstein between classes.

non-creased air force one sneakers   all white.

           blacktop ballad.

locker's turntable.

        ms. jacobs sings our names   we can't hear.

we freestyle—

     rhyme   *nigga* with *nigga.*

[freestyle: denoting a contest or version of a sport in which there are few restrictions on the moves or techniques that competitors use; freestyle rapping is spitting lyrics in ciphers (or alone) that you make up on the spot. while you might sneak in a line or two that you wrote the night before, most of your flow should be improvised, spontaneous, and off the top o' the dome.]

9th grade vernacular, aka skeet

skeet, a pseudo-archaic derivative of "shoot,"
understood by our dedication to lil jon
& the eastside boyz relentless contributions
to our 9th grade vernacular. omari insists

it was a synonym for pleasuring oneself,
while nana convinces the rest of us otherwise.
the time between debate was spent surveying
cyclical hips to all *skeet skeet motherfucker,*

which lent no hand in deciphering the code
that plagued the blacktop. soon, the ballad
that signaled co-ed dancing fell to bottom
of the billboard 100 as *drop it like it's hot*

rose like our bodies during homecoming dance.
here is what i remember: each body, a catalyst,
aiding in our unfailing quest, or scholarly
debate, to discover its meaning, *skeet*—

ways of pronouncing rapper, 2017

lil uzi vert,

madeintyo,

lil yachty,

      how they make the tongue polysyllabic.
stretching the way we wield our mouths to pronounce:

musician

an ecosystem
that sings our glory,
its grime and gospel.

what other way to sing autonomy?

what other way
      to sing,

than to break

our grammar

the way 808s shake

license plates loose

on the rears of big body

american cars.

how we say,

a boogie wit da hoodie,

& our minds retract all predictions

and become bilingual

three minutes at a time

as if to say

we are unscripted

—freestyle our names too.

mama gave her quvenzhané

gave her fifty cents to buy a quarter juice box
gave her a look when she tracked in dirt

> *you smell like outside*
> *get washed up before dinner*

gave her red beans and rice

> always gave her something to eat
> cheese puffs and a quarter juice box for dessert

gave her a belt when she found her window open

> *you musta' forgot*
> *falling from the second story'll hurt!*

gave her to christ
gave her quvenzhané.
gave her benediction
gave her stories

> Black mothers had nothing to give but names

gave her quvenzhané.

boulevard Black

legs that beat

        east 14th

used to beat boys

        in races on the block

and get beat blue

        for staying out after

lamp post becomes

        boulevard Black

the same way natasha's

        eye looked after

she got beat

flower poem

& ain't it like us to make dying
beautiful. ain't it like us to find
a way to make decay more
appealing. basquiat ~~crossed~~

out words so you would
see them more and here he is
at the helm of this dirt canvas.
sepia sprayed across each slab

staccato. & all these syllables
like ragweed exed. if my body
goes, pollinate each block
with my ashes. let each tongue

savor the spores, the names
crossed out like an aftertaste.

how to find waldo

always search for god
my stepfather tells me
after disappearing,
he comes. eyes a crimson
like two red giants
had colonized Black holes
that once held place there.
white residue on the
bathroom counter,
my mother in the next
room gasping for air.
he must have found god
in her neck   his hands
pressed her skin into
a blood blanched map.
his lips crimped shut,
yet leaking scripture.
as if to say,

    always search for god.

jr. drank his coffee Black

and by Black, i mean,
no shade other than his oil-slick
skin was allowed to get close

enough to share the same air.
if he was reading this he'd say,
that goes for dominoes,
checkerboards, cows, penguins,

zebras, soccer balls and cars too.
say, *white vehicles aren't allowed*
in the same lane on the highway.
say, *i got a double barrel and bail*

money for anyone who becomes
brave behind the wheel. jr speaks
only when spoken to, *sir & ma'am*
bookend each sentence unwieldy.

story goes: jr's battalion, a slew of white

boys wary of napalm, sent him into the
grey of the unknown to get confirmation

and jr drank his coffee Black since.

albany middle school teaches a lesson on entrepreneurship

our bookbags be a Black market—

        meager juveniles brandishing singles

behind blacktop filled fingernails

        and back-pockets void of wallets.

by nine, i break even. jamel pries

        open his second box of starburst, while

kumi brokers six bucks to a sixth grader

        for the lack of supply and huge demand.

half past noon, our surge

        comes to a halt, and we gather behind

the b building to compare profits

        and crack jokes on jamel's short shorts.

tuesday through thursday be the same saga.

        transactions in the hallways. while friday

be a sabbath, a space for us to take flight

        over the basketball courts with our nikes.

on sunday, costco be a kingpin

      that knew we'd never miss a re-up unless

ms. peggy called our mothers in for a meeting

      to discuss the school's drop in lunch sales.

monday be a chalk talk, our first lesson on

      the ways our brown bodies aren't allowed

to yield the same way other bodies are.

      aren't allowed to multiply the same.

by monsters, i mean, Black boys

monsters need not be present
        on key route boulevard
after midnight. clifton's hands
        at ten and two. the rest of us kill
        time by recalling our underaged club access
on our way home. *pay attention,* this is how it always
begins:

        our car, a sea of red and blue.
the basis, our 16-year-old Black bodies
        the weight of a badge,
flashlights blinding,
                clanking of cuffs
and knees that fill
        the creases in our backs

how to die after they've buried you

place your brown body in the small Black box,
    make an effort to do so quietly,

no riots or rage tonight.
    learn the muscle memory of smiling

then swallow the temptation. only mugs
    and shots allowed here. you can have

both for free. i once stole a zebra cake
    from 7-11 when i was nine by accident,

avoid eye contact, it may keep you alive
    avoid eye contact, avoid eye contact.

close your eyes. close your eyes. now—

we usually fought
before we knew why

as suburban as albany middle school was, nothing sang power like the faces of jamel, delroy, clifton, nana and i, as custom was to glue our Black bodies to each other in order to stay fist. our huddle, a fortress not to be tempted or broken.

●

one afternoon, clifton launched a kickball, which turned the courtyard into a civil war. nick's tongue infantry. our unmediated response was an inaugural war drum. a tempo racing as fast as our heartbeats. nick swung, then we fought like we were pennsylvania and a confederate was attempting to take our lunch money.

congregation

the second after untying
       our durag is a congregation.
the collective's thundering
       gasp,   it's benediction and stretched line
running
       from forehead to ear .

anticipatory rock
             and lean
             during an onset, the beat

everyone's a baritone — for big's sake,
       we, on cue,
           it was all a dream,
           i used to read word up! magazine
           salt-n-pepa and heavy d
           up in the limousine
(rap the rest
       instead of finishing this poem,
you started doing it anyway,
       — welcome to the congregation)

cupid shuffle isn't a line
       dance, but a congregation

we dancing, but ain't never
>   in a line, end up wherever
our shoes take us. spinning
>   twice more than the song says.
uncle so and so's hip
>   don't hurt today. body aint rebelling
today.
>   our hips are a congregation.

'got me fucked up
>   is a congregation, the same way
i wish a motherfucka would is,
both prayers or rhetorical devices
>   as if to say: we disagree,   but—

>   i got god on my side.

all trains gather
at macarthur

to taste jamaican fruit and hear
djembe around five thirty. after
the richmond line quiets
its screeches and millbrae

stands at attention

—lull—

turnstiles mix and master tickets. four
dialects of english spill down the escalator:
broken, self-righteous, exhausted and
otherwise proper. hips sway unknowingly to
drums, street vendors peak, crescendo. the
lady beside the clerk's window sang and
macarthur station dies again— for the
moment.

mongoose teaches
a lesson in linguistics

chauffeur

to another language

sludged-sprockets

evict the chain

each block

my four-city voyage

to school

clink and veer

empty scotch

perched below

my front tire

bottle colonized cart

half-erected tents

beneath the 880—

      dub: enough weed

      duby: the salvaged bit

      bust a knock: oblige an addict

chain—
trash bins
lined broadway
like guardrails
collecting all things
time neglected

    valet: trust

    four-in-hand necktie: white male

    taxi: good luck!

clink and veer

(caution, hidden driveways)
million-dollar coaches
down the hill, a cyclist

    venti: large

    dog park: playground for animals

    teacher: white female

arrive at school—
trilingual

jamaican food

brixton-london, summer 2016

as flies danced beneath the heat lamp,
i spoke. *two jerk chicken patties
and a slice of cocoa bread, but instead
of cabbage, rice and peas please.* i
watched as the busyness of her aged
brown hand halted. *you american, you
have accent*! flipping through the many
faces of queen elizabeth in my wallet, i
was reminded how far away from *home*
i was, so i conceded and handed her
a banknote. *keep the change?*

broken english

ahmed's english breaks
        after each word,

(a slight pause
of interrogation
as if discovering
each term mechanically)

perhaps
        it's his tongue re-
belling (colonialism,)
the way it spills
        its discourse
and expects you to pretend
there isn't mud trudged
through your home or
front door left open.

what happens to the mouth
        as it sculpts

a new language?

as the tongue finds
        new ways of ex-
pressing its distaste
for subjugation.
how each vowel becomes
malignant. how it breaks
english un
        evenly.
how ahmed pronounces
        his name
wrong now.

retribution

our fists became anchors
discovering new rage and braving
its shores as the yard monitor peeled
us from his body. at the time, i wished

it a corpse. i wished it an opposing
vessel sunk below the sea
of our smite. till this day, i have no idea
what possessed david to call us niggers,

or that it matters. suspension,
in-school, after our retribution, and
the occupancy of ms. peggy's office felt
like a block party, not a punishment.

during those seven-hour-a-day
sentences, we cracked jokes on jamel's
short shorts, and drank strawberry crush
soda out her fridge.

& bodies like david's never drown,
they just find new land to colonize.

baritone body

body—
breaking,

        Black bodies
body's   breaking
    beside gurneys
news,
     breaking news!

a body's been broke,

       Black
       boy
       baritone
       broken
       bronzed
       bucked
       bad
       brazen

       eulogy—   Black
          boy
          bad
            broken

bronzed
bucked
brazen
baritone

broken

breaking

bodies.

while the praise team sings how great,

anthony is crying// says
        he misses his father// says bullets
took his father hostage// music on sunday
        says: sometimes we shall sing
until the pain subsides// says
        we lost our song// says we Black
boys should sing our way to heaven
        or as aunt lotty says: *sang*// still,
he doesn't know how to listen
        to the gospel without his eyes
singing songs his heart
        wished it didn't know

the day after fruitvale

because oscar grant's killer hadn't been cuffed,
a volkswagen passat was in flames
outside my apartment window because
i lived uptown and the oakland police
station was two blocks away & because
folks care more about cars than bodies & because
my people know that, shit goes up in flame.

because our protest is mistaken for riot &
not peaceful, my people's eyes tend to tear,
gas fills our blocks & because
oscar laid in his own blood, my people lay
in front of cars on interstate 880 & because
folks care more about a commute than a community,
it's illegal to march on the highway & because
my people know that, they march on the highway.

because mourning is an empiricist on ecstasy &
words often lack sense, the crust of a stone in hand &
half-drunk molotov cocktail is the greatest feeling in
standoff with blue and Black & because
moms would've seen me on tv, i placed the amplifier
in my second story window instead & because
music sings in our name, my people sung
we gon' be alright on 23rd street.

concerning: kendrick and martin

i've been meaning to ask if

we gon' be alright is optimism or

a synonym for

endurance, like, when i was seven

& wanted to fly

i rode my power wheels down two flights

of stairs, my mouth a flask of blood

& my stepfather sung *we gon' be alright*

& i'm still not,

so i got stitches

instead. i wonder if i had let endurance have its way,

if i'd still have a tongue to pray with. tell me,

is *alright* passive the way mr. martin was

when he saw the mountain top?

what's the view like from there?

you say *we gon' be alright*

he says *we gon' make it*

to the promised land and i wonder

if this is it? if this *alright* is enough? no?

i figure you more of the malcolm type, k-dot,

tell me, are *we gon'*

be alright, because i have a daughter

now and i want her to grow old

enough to bury me

tell me, does the key pharrell sings *-right* in

endure the hi-hat the same way we do?

trying to dodge each stroke of the beater

or trill through it. is lucy endurable?

tell me, kendrick, are we

gon' be alright?

roosters in the hood

every home has a chest

      each chest flex on cue

each body hard

      every porch has a body

everybody live

      each day is a push up

a chest day

      a cockerel doing push ups

each block, a body

      every rooster, a chest

in the hood, everybody

a chest, a flex on cue

a crow, a rooster

in the hood, a home

a porch, a chest, a flex,

a crow—

an open letter to the police department

after the news of andrew kearse

playing dead is not a pastime,

not a way of claiming liberty, or

self-justice, or eluding your inevitable

force. when a Black body stops moving,

it is always already a blues-hit silenced

by a government that believes

died in police custody somehow—

makes murder sound less aggressive.

few feet separating loudonville and arbor hill

flowerpots in symmetry
lined the city limit. homes flex
their chests in unison. hamlet
years ago and still small in stature,
its single road and its start.

sun set on arbor hill
yesterday. wind gathered everything
weak enough to be uprooted
and ferried it to the highway rough
poor, or white collared.

tar was a melting pot
that knew no socio-economic
background. traffic flowed
in both directions with no repent
for the way the hill hugged
the guardrail to survive
the same way loudonville
used it as a baton.

summary of
martin luther king jr. way

oakland 1998

bar-b-que.	concrete.	bones or
dominoes.	trash talk.	garbage.
gutters.	gas.	gas pedal.
donuts.	intersection.	donut.
uncle ()'s driveway.	hopscotch.	heelies
chalk.	powder.	power.
nike.	nickels.	night.
powder.	panther.	wicker chair.
porch.	present.	regal.
race.	rage.	regal.
tank top.	blacktop.	Black top.

around the roundabout

inside 105th avenue's gaping mouth,

        each street spoke spanish,

el paseo, estapa, capistrano drive

    danced a dance

        that kept sobrante park nocturnal

       grupera—

the immense voice that

      sang its song

    through the screen door slits &

          backseat amplifiers

a perpetual ballad that dopeboys

     slung

       around the roundabout

revolving like samba.

ballad of our backyard
oakland 1998-2002

lips was always polite to mama:

always using *ma'am, please & thanks*

always side stepping next to my window

        always paranoid

always reaching into the tiny hole in our backyard

always pulling out bags of sugar when i was seven

always pulling out bags of cocaine when i was eleven

always hopping our back fence when sirens blared

always dying like others did when the competition spikes

always leaving without saying goodbye

always quiet by my bedroom window now

mary don't you weep teaches a lesson on revelations

martin luther king jr. blvd., west oakland, 2002

mama never leaves the front door open for fear of flies.

& how will this fear consume you?

a shudder and a shadow flash across the yard.

the smoke that tiptoed its way
                    around the bend
that didn't startle as much as the foreign howls.

& why was the door undone?

the somber roar, and smoke that colonized

the living room   disgorged my sister and me through
the front door only, to marvel at mother nature's boast—

a hall full of vapor   a hall full of flame

a boy that sleeps the dichotomy of this   one eye open.

deluge

i'll never forget watching
my aunt attempt to muster

        a water main break with

a single roll of paper towels

dripping with the same water

           our neighbors bathed

in earlier that night while
questioning how the only Black
folks on the block managed to

stay afloat for years.

house at 210 sunnyside avenue

after marcus jackson

house whose walls kept a man's tears
from spilling into the street every night.
house where a dinner table collected
both paper and dust, and rattled
from the deep of his throat.
reverberation down two flights of stairs,
the stilt stature. house we painted over
with faultless white paint.
its scars, beneath a veil of vigor
his four decades held hostage. house
not allowed to sleep in, on sunday.

      house that sang a sigh on escrow.
sang a recessional.

      house that sings   still.

zoology

i never understood how one could serve fifteen terms of life in prison without eating one's self alive from the hunger of daylight or how my cousin jonathan managed to mangle a sandwich in less than 60 seconds or why my mother decided to tell me her experience with milwaukee 1978 after i watched *hannibal* or how my uncle pete managed to survive the temptation of jeffrey dahmer's inevitable mouth. despite my confusion, my appetite always excavated itself during the rest stops on the six-hour greyhound bus ride from los angeles to oakland aboard the same coach a man was beheaded and eaten just a year before.

a song about death

leftover
>> storm water collects
>>>> below
the steps.
>> this body's appetite
planked
>> across the cement
and tentacles frisking
>> the ground for a taste
of moisture.

the sky colonized
>> by the sun
and its freckled glory.
>> the way it peeks cumulous
as if to say—
>> bury yourself
>> in the ground
>> once more before
i burn
you alive.

while in south west nine, london,

a man sells patties from a two-foot gap in the wall-

     steel drum plays itself

          a bouquet of smoke, both incense and pipe

another beat—

three for $10 my man, the time it takes to flag a backpacker

     below the overground bridge

blocks beside a mosque

        a synagogue rests in peace

when a people mourn

what more is there to a heartbeat
but a crescendo, eager to fill
the body's veins with enough
blood to jumpstart a motor city riot.

there is no blueprint for pain.

each time a prayer is said,
it is half psalm, half arrow.
as much blade as it is a promise
made between fingers to cut
anyone or anything attempting
to colonize the suffering.

in defense of specific

after hanif abdurraqib

arithmetic / y = mx+b / exam answer key / dna / 212⬛, the moment before
water becomes overzealous / christianity- / via dolorosa / 650 yards / path to
salvation / *thou shalt not kill,* sixth commandment / august 2, 1924, james
baldwin took his first breath / 128 pages in the *the fire next time* / 6 hours
it took to read both essays while on road trip from oakland, california to
portland, oregon / 65 mph speed limit on highway 101 / semantics / inhale /
exhale / the way the tongue hurls air out the mouth / an abdomen contracting
/ hand gesture / thumb / index finger / connected / "as if to say" / ways to
pronounce / *specific* / one / eight letters / three syllables.

[snow dissolves steady on her brow raised as she demands: pacific! as thick as her position, the stoop we sat on buried itself
and 106th street laid still, as did my posture, attempting to decode her tongue. the quarrel over the word: specific, left my
mouth lusting for the body of water she referred to. she'd never been to california or traveled the 101 while the sun was
setting. in gridlock, my timberland boots making beats on the concrete below them, each of us unmoved, blizzard mid-
april. i concede.]

ecdysis

space between
    his shoulders

makes a mosaic
    brown, bloody

and the kind of pink
    that reveals itself

on playgrounds after
    jumping from the swing

in midair.
    don't scratch:

instruction,
    how his skin

was didactic,
    showing each reader

the differences
    in terrain, be it

vast dry land
       or tropical from the way

fingernails wrecked
       the ecosystem.

calamine in palms,
       oatmeal in water,

him singing praise
       to them both,

despite genetics
       telling him to shed.

around the roundabout

one entrance to sobrante park

      past the ten-foot tented fence that

         keeps the once-alive swing set

               and two-foot

                    dark blue slide at bay

children ride their tricycles

         up and down edes street

                       kept safe

        by the self-elected

         heavily armed watchmen

             that have an equal chance

                of shooting

       as they do

         whistling at anyone

         or anything

             entering the roundabout

               without permission

praise dance

her hands praised the air
        a mosaic in progress   i watched

feet jump to—
           baptist clap cues
      and the church
mother's routine *hallelujah*!

baby bouncing atop papa's knees

his cadence-
        drummers drum and
                the church
mother's *hallelujah*.

          balancé
once more

music halts   its horns,

a wingtip kicks the podium

& her conversation

         with god
abrupt.

the smell of kevin's belch

kevin devoured
　　　　everything but
marrow,
　　　　would chew
bone if he had strong
　　　　enough jaws
and a bottomless
　　　　appetite to swallow
dinnertime whole

　　　　it didn't stop
him from trying
　　　　each night, his
body's language
　　　　for masculinity,
its tight grip,
　　　　constant hunger.

the way he used
　　　　his tongue to spit—
both scripture
　　　　and the taste
of tobacco

coffee

mama's a fan of clawfoot tubs.
        chipped white paint
and a silver stain ring inside.
        she soaks every night
until her skin buckles.

corroded red and Black kettle screams
        for attention while she towels
off. in go two and a half scoops
        of sugar and an eyeballed
splash of half and half.

teaspoon spins until she reaches
        the nightstand holding
up a king james and ragged journal.

half of psalms until her eyes
        no longer strain the Black
and white. her coffee prays
        a lukewarm lullaby.

morning yanks the drapes
        to a half-drunk cup,
hurried mother,

a '95 gold volvo warming
up in the driveway and a damp
mat inside the bathroom—

notes on alice

several years after her death, there was much fuss about whether her name
was *alice* or *alma*.

♦

at the time of her birth, Black folk' names carried as much weight as all of
their wages for sharecropping combined.

♦

as the story goes: the midwife couldn't transcribe and wrote *alma* instead
of *alice*.

♦

she was the cynosure and turret of the 14 of them. grew up under the clench
of teenage big brothers and the oil and water that was mississippi in the
1930's.

♦

when she became a mother, she owned a cast-iron skillet. used it as a thick
Black fist at the first sight of disagreement. then, placed the unimpaired
skillet on the stove to make breakfast for her eight children. my mother,
second youngest of them.

◆

her bifocals thick enough to penetrate each attempt at dishonesty. not quite
five feet, but tall enough to reach the pot rack.

◆

mama has her almond shaped eyes, as do i. she cuts them at the first sign of
disagreement. grandma would be proud of the woman she's become. cooks a
mean pot of tuscan soup, and owns a cast iron skillet.

the day the roundabout stood still,

grandfather's gray astro van leisured

beneath a ripe tree, collecting all

the reddish-orange, less-sour mandarins

our seven-year-old arms couldn't reach

while he, who always pushed his own chair,

destined for his market-visit lay

wrecked below the wheels of a city cab,

the way a newborn lay moments after

birth. his wheelchair two body-lengths

away, crushed beneath neglect

of a driver & sobrante park lay still

full of rotting fruits. while we prayed

today's prayer

my son, tell them the body is a blade that sharpens by cutting.

-ocean vuong

today's prayer is for honing steel,
a third testament that Black folks anchor

to their galvanized body in ink. today's
prayer is for a radical revision. in this variation,

jesus grew up in oakland off seminary
and oakland don't have two cheeks. after

the first, you'll discover how sharp Black
can be. in this variation, simon, andrew

and john are angela, eldridge and huey.
today's prayer is for honing steel and a chopping

block. today's prayer is for peer review—
today's prayer is to revise and resubmit.

today's prayer doesn't include
submission. today's prayer is broadcast

from calvary and longinus didn't get the good
side. in this variation we don't lose blood,

just dull shrapnel. today's prayer is for a blade.
today's prayer is for a self-sharpening body.

concerning: nylon

Black boys love
their mothers too
much to die
in front of them,
willingly.

concerning: sandra

now Black mothers teach
their babies revelations before
they learn them genesis
and pray they live
       to see the gospels
in between.

urban dictionary
says daniel

is a Black boy or   block boy   or   is a Black & block boy

and still is a poem   with complexity   and extended metaphor

that does not include   prisoner   or   junkie   or

anything not   self-proclaimed   the way stigma always seems to

auto-fill itself   is blade   is rebellion   by breathing

is   nigga   pronounced [nigg- ah]

depending on the day   is a gibson les paul between

muddy waters' fingers   sweaty, yet triumphant

is a chicago blues hall in the 40's   is enough   grace

to catcall tomorrow   like it was some sort of courtship

is a swollen belly   is hunger   is the smell of hunger

        a plastic spatula left on the stove   or baking soda

& hot water   is hot water   just before it boils

[mama gave me a biblical name. one that means: god is my judge, or in other words, there ain't a person walking earth with enough holy in their body to try and break its cadence. one that means: you will bury me one day, but before my song comes to a close, i will call you by your name and nothing else— i will call you by your name, it has always been enough.]

NOTES

- **divine, divine, divine** borrows a line from langston hughes' "i, too"

- **the day after fruitvale** borrows a line from kendrick lamar's "alright"

- **9th grade vernacular** quotes a part of the hook of lil john and the east side boyz' "get low"

- the title, **another negro burned** comes from a new york times headline from 1983 in which henry smith was lynched

- **congregation** includes lyrics from the notorious big's "juicy"

acknowledgments

This book would not be possible without the encouragement, editing and love from the homie, Quintin Collins, and the whole Solstice MFA program, where many of these poems were birthed. Thank you to my mentors: Nicole Terez Dutton, Iain Haley Pollock, Kathleen Aguero, Dzvinia Orlowsky, and Laure-Anne Bosselaar, for your care and attention. Thank you to those who workshopped and wrestled with these poems at any stage. Thank you to the many folks who inspired conversations or thoughts that lead to this work: D.Colin, Daniella Toosie-Watson, Michael McGee Jr., Jamel Freeman, Nkateko Masinga, and Lebogang Mashile.

Thank you to my late grandfather, Bernard Clemons, who gives me courage to write. Thank you to my sister, Tenesha Smith, and my 9th grade english teacher, Mr. Ross. Both of you are the reasons I picked up a pen. Thank you to my family: sisters, nieces, nephews, especially those who make appearances in these poems.

Much appreciation to J. K. Fowler for believing in this collection and giving it a home at Nomadic Press. Much love to the folks of Nomadic Press who spent countless hours editing and preparing this book for the world: Noelia Cerna, Michaela Mullin,and Jevohn Newsome.

Big ups to Amen'auset Shotlow-Turner for the dope cover illustration and bringing my ideas to fruition.

Shoutout to Oakland and all of its grime and glory for making me and making these poems.

Finally, the warmest thank you to my beloved, Quianna, for your unwavering support and love.

Additionally, word to the following journals and publications for giving earlier versions of these poems a home:

A Garden of Black Joy Anthology: "ways of pronouncing rapper"
Califragile: "jr drank his coffee black," "broken english," "baritone body" and "dialects of praise"
Cogs: "all of the others seek refuge here" and "how to die after they've buried you"
Cosmonauts Avenue: "mongoose teaches a lesson in linguistics," "pledge teaches a lesson on loyalty" and "the day after fruitvale"
Monterey County Weekly: "open letter to the police department"
Obsidian: "congregation" and "kumi & i freestyle"
Streetlight Press: "shakespeare teaches a lesson on loyalty" and "ecdysis"
The Hellebore: "aunt georgia makes fried chicken" and "albany middle school teaches a lesson on entrepreneurship"
The Lilly Review: "around the roundabout"
Trampset: "concerning fire"

classroom guide

Theme: Grief/Loss

Loss is an experience that most people face unfortunately. Most of the time, there is nothing that will "fix" loss, but there are ways to help cope with or make sense of it. One thing that people turn to is music! Which begs the question, how can music help support us in our times of loss or grief?

PROMPTS

1. Consider a time or period when you were experiencing grief or loss and jot down some of the names of songs that you listened to during that time. Next, think of either the chorus or a line from the songs you wrote down and use it as a jumping off point for a focused 10 minute freewrite. Once you're done, read through what you came up with and underline or highlight keywords or phrases that speak to the loss or grief you were experiencing. Use these words or phrases to write a poem about grief or loss.

2. Grab a verse from one of your favorite songs. Take a moment to analyze and think about what the verse is attempting to say. Then write a poem in response to that verse as a letter directly addressed to the artist who wrote/performed the song.

"the day after fruitvale"

"concerning: kendrick and martin"

"while the praise team sings how great"

♦

Theme: Community

Community by definition has to do with living within close proximity to one another or sharing common characteristics; however, community can also be built through shared experiences and shared triumphs. In fact, communities that are built through collective struggle or collective experience are often stronger in nature. Additionally, you may build community through common celebration or interests.

PROMPTS

1. Think about a time in life when you shared a challenge with friends. Consider the way you and everyone else coped with the challenge. Did you all talk about the challenge? Did you provide support to each other? In retrospect, what is it that helped you during the challenge? What do you know now about the situation that would have helped while you were dealing with it? After answering these questions, write a poem to you and your friends capturing the challenge and what you know to be true now about the situation as the last line.

"albany middle school teaches a lesson on entrepreneurship"

2. Consider all the ways you and your friends are connected. What are the shared interests? What are the shared philosophies or ideas? What is the glue that keeps you in community with them? Make a list of all of these items. Use the list to write a poem about your communal relationship and all the things that glue you together.

REPRESENTATIVE POEM(S):

"congregation"

♦

Theme: Nostalgia

Oftentimes we get caught up in the narrative of life and forget the moments that have brought us joy. Nostalgia is one way that remembering joy manifests itself in the narrative of our trials and tribulations. Let's explore nostalgia!

PROMPT

1. Make a list of items or places that brought you joy as a child or teen. Try and use words or phrases that appeal to the senses (taste, touch, smell, hearing, sight). Now rearrange the list to tell an autobiographical story. Start the earliest object, item or place and

then continue chronologically. Don't worry about making "sense," just place words or phrases in the correct order. Lastly, title your poem something that tells the reader what they are looking at. For example, "my time as a 12 year old" or "life at Oakland High."

REPRESENTATIVE POEM(S):

"summary of martin luther king jr. way"

Daniel B. Summerhill

Daniel B. Summerhill is a poet, performance artist and scholar from Oakland, California. He received an MFA in creative writing from Solstice of Pine Manor College. His work has been published in *Obsidian, Rust + Moth, Cogs, The Hellebore, Gumbo, The Lilly Review,* and elsewhere. He lives on California's central coast and is Assistant Professor of Poetry/Social Action and Composition Studies at California State University Monterey Bay.

OTHER WAYS TO SUPPORT NOMADIC PRESS' WRITERS

In 2020, two funds geared specifically toward supporting our writers were created: the **Nomadic Press Black Writers Fund** and the **Nomadic Press Emergency Fund.**

The former is a forever fund that puts money directly into the pockets of our Black writers. The latter provides up to $200 dignity-centered emergency grants to any of our writers in need.

Please consider supporting these funds. You can also more generally support Nomadic Press by donating to our general fund via nomadicpress.org/donate and by continuing to buy our books. As always, thank you for your support!

Scan here for more information and/or to donate.
You can also donate at nomadicpress.org/store.